EYEWITNESS TO HISTORY

CESAR CHAVEZ

in his own words

Gareth Stevens
PUBLISHING

By Sarah Machajewski

Please visit our website, www.garethstevens.com. For a free color catalog of all our high-quality books, call toll free 1-800-542-2595 or fax 1-877-542-2596.

Library of Congress Cataloging-in-Publication Data

Machajewski, Sarah, author.
 Cesar Chavez in his own words / Sarah Machajewski.
     pages cm. — (Eyewitness to history)
 Includes index.
ISBN 978-1-4824-4090-4 (pbk.)
ISBN 978-1-4824-4059-1 (6 pack)
ISBN 978-1-4824-4060-7 (library binding)
1. Chavez, Cesar, 1927-1993. 2. Migrant agricultural laborers—United States—Biography. I. Title. II. Series: Eyewitness to history (Gareth Stevens Publishing)
 HD1525.M224 2016
 331.88'13092—dc23
 [B]

                                    2015028098

First Edition

Published in 2016 by
Gareth Stevens Publishing
111 East 14th Street, Suite 349
New York, NY 10003

Copyright © 2016 Gareth Stevens Publishing

Designer: Katelyn E. Reynolds
Editor: Therese Shea

Photo credits: Cover, p. 1 (Cesar Chavez) Dave Buresh/The Denver Post via Getty Images; cover, pp. 1 (background image), 13, 25 Cathy Murphy/Getty Images; cover, p. 1 (logo quill icon) Seamartini Graphics Media/Shutterstock.com; cover, p. 1 (logo stamp) YasnaTen/Shutterstock.com; cover, p. 1 (color grunge frame) DmitryPrudnichenko/Shutterstock.com; cover, pp. 1–32 (paper background) Nella/Shutterstock.com; cover, pp. 1–32 (decorative elements) Ozerina Anna/Shutterstock.com; pp. 1–32 (wood texture) Reinhold Leitner/Shutterstock.com; pp. 1–32 (open book background) Elena Schweitzer/Shutterstock.com; pp. 1–32 (bookmark) Robert Adrian Hillman/Shutterstock.com; p. 5 Tony Korody/The LIFE Images Collection/Getty Images; pp. 7, 8, 9, 11 courtesy of Library of Congress; p. 15 BarbaraAlper/Getty Images; p. 17 (flag) Aztecas Califas/Wikipedia.org; pp. 17 (image), 19, 21 Arthur Schatz/The LIFE Picture Collection/Getty Images; p. 23 Photo by MichaelRougier/The LIFE Picture Collection/Getty Images; p. 27 Bob Parent/Hulton Archive/Getty Images.

Printed in the United States of America

CPSIA compliance information: Batch #CW16GS: For further information contact Gareth Stevens, New York, New York at 1-800-542-2595.

CONTENTS

*Words in the glossary appear in **bold** type the first time they are used in the text.*

A VOICE
for Millions

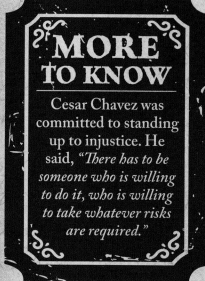

MORE TO KNOW

Cesar Chavez was committed to standing up to injustice. He said, *"There has to be someone who is willing to do it, who is willing to take whatever risks are required."*

The history of agriculture in the United States is one of hardship for the men and women who have worked the land. From an agricultural economy based on slavery in the pre–Civil War South to the millions of migrant workers who toil in fields today, farm labor in the United States has rarely been kind to its workers. In the 1960s, one person became the voice of a movement that worked to create better conditions for farm laborers. That man was Cesar Chavez.

As a boy from a family of migrant workers (and later one himself), Chavez knew firsthand the injustices farm laborers faced. His tireless **activism** brought national attention to the dangers of farmwork. His dedication and message of nonviolence earned the support of millions. This is his story.

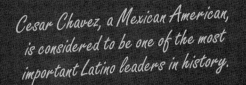

Cesar Chavez, a Mexican American, is considered to be one of the most important Latino leaders in history.

WHAT IS A PRIMARY SOURCE?

This book uses primary sources to tell Cesar Chavez's story. Primary sources are documents or objects that were created during a time of history. They include speeches, letters, interviews, artwork, objects, and more. Primary sources are important because they give us a powerful sense of history, allowing us to study it through the eyes of people who lived it. By understanding Cesar Chavez's own words, we can better know the man behind the movement that changed history.

GROWING UP
During the Great Depression

WHAT WAS THE GREAT DEPRESSION?

The Great Depression was a time of great economic suffering around the world. In October 1929, the US stock market crashed. Banks and businesses lost millions of dollars. By 1933, over 16 million Americans were unemployed. With no work and no money, they were unable to buy food for their families. Millions of families, like Cesar's, lost their homes and their businesses. The terrible suffering forced many people to move in search of work, which meant leaving behind everything they knew.

Cesar Chavez was born March 31, 1927, near Yuma, Arizona. He was named after his grandfather, who **immigrated** to Arizona from Mexico in the 1880s. Cesar was the second-oldest child in a family with six children. His parents owned a ranch and ran a small store.

When Cesar was young, his family had enough money to live comfortably. However, his father was cheated by an Anglo, or white, landowner, which hurt the Chavez family financially. At the same time, the Great Depression had taken hold in the United States. Chavez remembered, *"[The Great Depression] . . . meant nothing to me then, but [was] a condition that would deeply scar* our lives, *despite my father's hard work.*" Cesar's family didn't have money to pay the taxes on their land and business. They lost them both.

States in the western and central part of the United States were hit with severe droughts, or long periods of no rain, during the 1930s. The land dried up and became unworkable. Farmers were already suffering because of the Depression and were often forced to leave their land.

MORE TO KNOW

When Cesar's relatives lost their jobs during the Great Depression, his father gave them **credit** from his store even though they couldn't pay it back. Eventually, the loss of goods and lack of money forced his father to lose his store.

LEAVING *Home*

MORE TO KNOW

In the 1930s, about 1.3 million Americans migrated to California in search of work.

When Cesar was 10 years old, the **impoverished** Chavez family moved to California to pick crops on farms. Migrant families moved from place to place following crops that were in season. Cesar once recalled, *"I can't remember our other migrant years as well as the first two. As we moved around, they blurred. The crops changed and we kept moving. There was a time for planting, and a time for thinning, and an endless variety of harvests up and down the state."*

This is an example of the kind of home many Mexican migrant workers lived in.

His family first lived in La Colonia **Barrio** in Oxnard, California. Then they moved to a barrio called "Sal Si Puedes," which means "get out if you can" in Spanish. Crowded, dirty, and without electricity or running water, conditions in these places were poor. In the 1940s, the family settled in Delano, California.

Migrant families packed their belongings into cars or wagons and set out in search of work.

NO TIME FOR SCHOOL

Chavez attended school through eighth grade. After his father was injured in an accident, the rest of the family had to start working. Cesar had wanted to go to high school, but it wasn't possible. *"No one had to tell me how bad off we were . . . . It was an automatic thing for me to say, 'I'll go to work, and I'll go to high school in two years.' But I never got there . . . . It's an economic reason entirely."* This was a common fate for migrant children.

BACKBREAKING *Work*

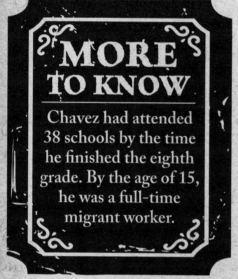
Life was hard for migrant workers. Picking crops was backbreaking work. Chavez often spoke of its physical effects. He remembered the skin on his hands splitting from picking crops, back pain, sore fingers, and more. Workers were exposed to **pesticides** and extreme heat. *"Many things in farm labor are terrible,"* he said. *"They should find a way of doing this work that will leave the human being whole."*

Workers were paid by how many crops they picked or how many acres they covered, so they had to work quickly. But they weren't paid much. In 1933, for example, some growers offered 60 cents for picking 100 pounds (45 kg) of cotton. Chavez always tried to find ways to make the work easier and faster for his family. *"We had to [finish] that acre,"* he said.

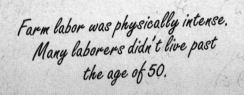

Farm labor was physically intense. Many laborers didn't live past the age of 50.

THE BRACERO PROGRAM

Launched in 1942, the Bracero Program brought more than 4 million Mexican farmworkers to the United States. When they arrived, they faced **discrimination**. White growers took advantage of Mexican laborers, paying them less than whites. Workers often didn't understand their contracts, which were written in English. Many were forced to return to Mexico as soon as their contracts expired. The Bracero Program was responsible for what many considered to be human rights abuses. It ended in 1964.

CHAVEZ'S
Education Begins

In 1946, at 17, Chavez left farmwork for the US Navy. After 2 years, he returned home. He married Helen Favela, and they moved to San Jose, California. Together they had seven children.

While in San Jose, Chavez met Father Donald McDonnell, a priest at the local Catholic church. *"My education started when I met Father McDonnell,"* Chavez said. Through McDonnell, Chavez learned about St. Francis of Assisi and Mahatma Gandhi and their belief in nonviolence as a force for change. Later, when Chavez himself became an activist, nonviolence was at the core of his message.

NONVIOLENCE AND CIVIL DISOBEDIENCE

Civil disobedience is the act of refusing to obey rules, laws, or commands put in place by a government or other organization. Usually, civil disobedience is associated with nonviolent resistance. This means using methods that don't hurt people, such as sit-ins, protests, **boycotts**, and fasts, to achieve change. This philosophy was made famous by Mahatma Gandhi, a man who used nonviolent resistance to help end British rule in India. His teachings inspired many activists in the United States.

McDonnell and Chavez also talked of the injustices farmworkers faced. McDonnell taught Chavez about unfair legislation and the striking difference between how workers and growers lived.

Family and faith were very important to Chavez. Both provided the foundation and support he needed to begin his life as an activist for social change.

MORE TO KNOW

"When we apply Gandhi's philosophy of nonviolence, it really forces us to think, really forces us to work hard. But it has power. It attracts the support of the people," Chavez wrote.

MEETING
Fred Ross

FIRST FIGHT

Chavez's first task as an organizer was voter registration, and it wasn't easy. Political groups in California put rules in place that said organizers could only register voters during daylight hours. They couldn't work on Sundays and couldn't speak Spanish when they were registering. On voting days, the political groups used **intimidation** at the polls. These actions made it difficult for Mexican Americans to vote. Chavez said it was his *"first fight with this power structure."*

Chavez knew how unfair conditions were for farm laborers. He knew they had to change, but how? In 1952, Chavez met Fred Ross, a man who would give him the tools he needed to turn his ideas into actions.

Fred Ross was a member of the Community Service Organization (CSO). This group aided underserved people. In the Los Angeles area, the CSO helped thousands of Mexican Americans gain citizenship and register to vote. It also fought police brutality and discrimination.

As Chavez listened to Ross, he became inspired: *"[Ross] did such a good job of explaining how poor people could build power that I could even taste it . . . I saw him organize, and I wanted to learn."*

Fred Ross's simple rules for organizing and bringing about change made sense to Chavez. Chavez said, "It's like digging a hole. There's nothing complicated about it." Ross is pictured here.

MORE TO KNOW

Chavez quickly rose through the ranks of the CSO. He became its director in 1958.

FOUNDING
the NFWA

Working for the CSO put Chavez on the path to finding his life's work: becoming a voice for migrant workers. Migrant workers were desperately poor, often couldn't understand

MORE TO KNOW

In 1963, it cost $42 a year for a family to join the NFWA. For impoverished migrant workers, this was a heavy cost to bear.

English, and lacked the tools to organize themselves. Chavez thought he could organize a union that worked on their behalf. This organization would fight for better wages and working conditions. It would also offer social services to its members. Chavez brought this idea to the CSO, but they rejected it. In 1962, he left the organization.

Chavez cofounded the National Farm Workers Association (NFWA) with Dolores Huerta, a former CSO organizer. Chavez and Huerta worked tirelessly to grow their union. Chavez received no pay until the NFWA had enough money to operate. By 1964, it had 1,000 members.

The NFWA's flag featured a black eagle in the center. The eagle symbolized the pride and **dignity** of its workers.

Cesar Chavez

Dolores Huerta

STARTING A REVOLT

When the CSO resisted Chavez's idea of unionizing farmworkers, he drew attention to his cause: *"I refused to sit at the head table at meetings, refused to wear a suit and tie . . . . At every meeting I got up and gave my standard speech: we shouldn't meet in fancy motels, we were getting away from the people, farmworkers had to be organized. But nothing happened. In March of '62 I resigned."*

The GRAPE
Strike Begins

As the NFWA grew, it started supporting small strikes around California. In 1965, the NFWA joined a strike of workers who picked roses, which resulted in a 120 percent wage increase. It also helped a small group of striking grape pickers.

In 1965, the Agricultural Workers Organizing Committee (AWOC), another union, launched a strike when Delano grape growers cut wages during the harvest. When the NFWA joined the AWOC, it became a strike made up of largely Chicanos, or people of Mexican descent.

In 1966, Chavez said, *"It is bigger . . . than just a strike. And if this spirit grows within the farm labor movement, one day we can use the force that we have to help correct a lot of things that are wrong in this society."*

WHAT IS A STRIKE?

A strike is when employees refuse to work as a form of protest, usually in order to gain something from their employer. This can be an effective way of protesting. When people strike, work may stop and employers lose money. Strikers often form lines in front of their place of employment, holding signs and declaring what they want. Sometimes, strikes are met with violence. The NFWA was committed to staying nonviolent, even when they were threatened.

Grape growers brought in strikebreakers—also known as scabs—to work while the strike continued. These people sometimes didn't know why the strike was happening. NFWA members often convinced them to leave the fields, and many ended up joining the cause.

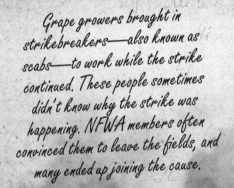

MORE TO KNOW

By September 1965, workers from more than 30 grape farms had decided to strike.

A MESSAGE
of Nonviolence

The Delano grape strikers employed unusual **tactics** for a labor strike. Under Chavez's leadership, the movement became known for its nonviolence. Workers didn't fight back even when violence was used against them.

When people saw strikers not fight back when they were hurt—or worse, killed—they became sympathetic. *"Nonviolence has the power to attract people and to generate power,"* Chavez said. *"By and large, people oppose violence. So when government or growers use violence against us, we strategize around it. We can respond nonviolently, because that swings people to our side, and that gives us our strength."*

Chavez's message struck a chord with people. Hundreds of students, church groups, activist groups, and everyday people joined the migrant workers' fight. In a few short years, the Delano grape strike had national support.

Chavez once gave a speech in which he said, "Once social change begins, it cannot be reversed. You cannot uneducate the person who has learned to read. You cannot humiliate the person who feels pride. And you cannot oppress the people who are not afraid anymore."

UNITED FOR A UNION

Some growers agreed to increase wages, but Chavez's ultimate goal was to unionize laborers. A union could bring change across farms. Most importantly, a union could secure a contract for better wages and working conditions. However, growers rejected this idea. In a speech during the strike, Chavez proclaimed, *"Our strike will stop every way the grower makes money until we have a union contract that guarantees us a fair share of the money he makes from our work!"*

BOYCOTTING
Grapes

In 1968, a 25-day water-only fast put Chavez and the strike in the national spotlight. People urged him to eat. But for Chavez, social justice could only be won through personal sacrifice. At the end of his fast, too weak to speak, he issued a statement: *"I am convinced that the truest act of courage . . . is to sacrifice ourselves for others in a totally nonviolent struggle for justice. To be a man is to suffer for others."*

Chavez became the face and voice of the Delano grape strike. He came up with many tactics to keep the nation's attention on the workers' cause. One of the most historic was the grape boycott. In 1968, Chavez asked people nationwide to stop buying grapes to show their support for migrant workers. If people didn't buy grapes, growers wouldn't make money. Growers would be forced to **negotiate**.

The grape boycott proved that even the smallest action could lead to great change. It brought the farmworkers' cause into millions of everyday people's homes. *"To us the boycott of grapes was the most near-perfect of nonviolent struggles. The boycott demonstrated to the whole country, the whole world, what people can do by nonviolent action,"* Chavez said.

MORE TO KNOW

At its peak, over 14 million Americans supported the grape boycott. Chavez said, *"We have witnessed truckloads of grapes being dumped because no one would stop to buy them. As demand drops, so do prices and profits. The growers are under tremendous economic pressure."*

Chavez's message of nonviolence drew the support of many important leaders, including Senator Robert F. Kennedy. This picture was taken on the final day of Chavez's 1968 fast.

LA CAUSA *Wins*

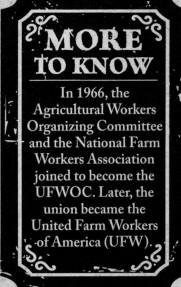

MORE TO KNOW

In 1966, the Agricultural Workers Organizing Committee and the National Farm Workers Association joined to become the UFWOC. Later, the union became the United Farm Workers of America (UFW).

The Delano grape strike lasted 5 years. On July 20, 1970, under increasing economic and social pressure, grape growers in California gave in. Twenty-six growers agreed to sign contracts with the United Farm Workers Organizing Commission (UFWOC). The union contracts guaranteed higher wages, health insurance benefits, and better working conditions for farm laborers. Chavez and La Causa had won.

Chavez also succeeded in another way. His efforts made people aware of the inequalities migrant workers faced. It was a step in the direction of changing how society operated. In an interview conducted in 1970, Chavez was asked what it would take to achieve the kind of society he envisioned. He said, *"It isn't the rule or the procedure or the ideology, but it's human beings that will make it."*

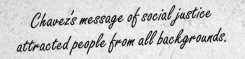

Chavez's message of social justice attracted people from all backgrounds.

EMPOWERMENT

Chavez, the UFWOC, and the Delano grape strike helped migrant workers, but it also helped Mexican Americans, a group that experienced much discrimination. As Chavez emerged as a powerful leader and activist, he empowered Latinos to have a voice. Mexican Americans rallied around the UFWOC, the organization that worked on their behalf. They had voting power and political weight. Many historians believe Chavez began a wave of Latino activism. Since Chavez's time, thousands of Latino leaders have held public office.

The FIGHT
Isn't Over

Despite the UFW's successes, behind the scenes, some growers were still working against laborers. In 1972, California lettuce growers entered into a deal with the Western Conference of Teamsters union in which the Teamsters agreed to represent lettuce pickers. However, the workers had no say in the matter. They didn't choose this representation, and the Teamsters didn't work for their best interests. Workers were angry.

Chavez and the UFW took action. They organized workers who wanted to unionize on their own. They called for a lettuce boycott and encouraged a strike.

¡SI SE PUEDE!

In 1972, the state of Arizona passed a law that prevented farmworkers from striking or boycotting during harvest seasons. Chavez underwent another fast, which landed him in the hospital. When a group of Latino leaders visited Chavez, they told him lawmakers and growers were too powerful to fight. *"It can't be done,"* they said. Chavez responded: *"¡Si, si se puede!"* which meant *"Yes, yes we can!"* The UFW adopted the saying for its campaigns.

In 1975, a landmark law passed in California that greatly helped the cause. The Agricultural Labor Relations Act granted farm laborers the right to **collective bargaining**. When farmworkers voted in the 1977 union election, they chose the UFW for representation.

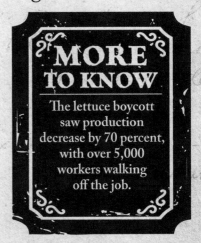

MORE TO KNOW

The lettuce boycott saw production decrease by 70 percent, with over 5,000 workers walking off the job.

In 1977, an interviewer from SOJOURNERS magazine asked Chavez where his power and determination came from. "I think it is my responsibility to do whatever I can," he said.

SERVING *Others*

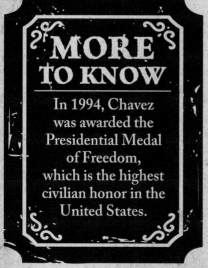

MORE TO KNOW

In 1994, Chavez was awarded the Presidential Medal of Freedom, which is the highest civilian honor in the United States.

Chavez continued to lead marches for better wages and working conditions. In the 1980s, he drew attention to the use of pesticides on grapes. Pesticides were very harmful for workers. Chavez called for another grape boycott in 1987. In 1988, he held a 36-day fast, which permanently damaged his health. But Chavez never stopped working. He died in Arizona in 1993. He was there to defend the UFW against a grower who filed a lawsuit against the organization. More than 35,000 people attended his funeral.

In just 15 years, Cesar Chavez transformed from a disadvantaged migrant worker into a powerful activist. He dedicated his life to improving others' lives, and his successes were historic. Today, he's remembered as one of the most important leaders in US history.

TIMELINE
THE LIFE OF CESAR CHAVEZ

1927 — Cesar Chavez is born near Yuma, Arizona, on March 31.

1929 — The Great Depression hits the United States.

1938 — The Chavez family moves from Arizona to California.

1946 — Chavez joins the US Navy.

1952 — Chavez meets Father Donald McDonnell and Fred Ross. Chavez joins the Community Service Organization (CSO) as an organizer.

1958 — Chavez becomes the director of the CSO.

1962 — Chavez leaves the CSO. He cofounds the National Farm Workers Association.

1965 — The Delano grape strike begins.

1968 — Chavez fasts for the first time in support of the strike.

1970 — Grape growers agree to union contracts with the United Farm Workers Organizing Committee.

1972 — California lettuce growers ask the Teamsters union to represent lettuce pickers. Chavez and the United Farm Workers of America (UFW) call for a boycott.

1975 — California's Agricultural Labor Relations Act grants farmworkers the right to collective bargaining.

1977 — Lettuce pickers elect the UFW as their union.

1987 — Chavez calls for a nationwide boycott of grapes to protest pesticides.

1988 — Chavez fasts for 36 days to bring attention to the pesticide problem.

1993 — Chavez dies in Arizona. Tens of thousands of people attend his funeral.

FOR A BETTER WORLD

In 1989, Chavez gave a speech in Tacoma, Washington, in which he spoke about his fast. He explained that one reason for his fast was *"for those who know that they could or should do more—for those who, by not acting, become bystanders in the poisoning of our food and the people who produce it."* At the end of his speech, he held all people accountable. *"The answer lies with you and me,"* he said. *"It is with all men and women who share the suffering and yearn with us for a better world."*

GLOSSARY

activism: a practice that stresses direct action to support or oppose one side of an issue

barrio: a Spanish-speaking part of a town or city

boycott: the refusal to buy something or do something as a protest

collective bargaining: talks between an employer and the leaders of a union about how a group of workers will be treated

credit: money that a bank or business will allow a person to use and then pay back in the future

dignity: the quality of being worthy of honor or respect

discrimination: the practice of unfairly treating a person or group of people differently from other people or groups of people

immigrate: to come to live permanently in a foreign country

impoverished: poor

intimidation: having to do with frightening someone in order to make them do what you want

negotiate: to discuss something formally in order to make an agreement

pesticide: a substance used for destroying bugs or other creatures that are harmful to plants or animals

tactic: an action or method that is planned and used to achieve a goal

FOR MORE
Information

Books

Carlson Berne, Emma. *What's Your Story, Cesar Chavez?* Minneapolis, MN: Lerner Publications, 2015.

Gregory, Josh. *Cesar Chavez*. New York, NY: Children's Press, 2015.

Stavans, Ilan. *Cesar Chavez: A Photographic Essay*. El Paso, TX: Cinco Puntos Press, 2010.

Websites

Cesar Chavez
www.americaslibrary.gov/aa/chavez/aa_chavez_subj.html
The Library of Congress offers valuable resources for students to learn about Cesar Chavez and his activism.

Cesar E. Chavez (1927–1993)
chavez.cde.ca.gov/ModelCurriculum/Teachers/Lessons/Resources/Biographies/Biographical_Sketch_4thGrd.aspx
The state of California provides a biography on Cesar Chavez.

INDEX